Piano Moments

100 Reflections That Can Make Your Life Better

MARK PAULSON

Photographs by Sondra Paulson

WESTBOW
PRESS®
A DIVISION OF THOMAS NELSON
& ZONDERVAN

WestBow Press books may be ordered through booksellers or by contacting:

WestBow Press
A Division of Thomas Nelson & Zondervan
1663 Liberty Drive
Bloomington, IN 47403
www.westbowpress.com
1 (866) 928-1240

Because of the dynamic nature of the Internet, any web addresses or links contained in this book may have changed since publication and may no longer be valid. The views expressed in this work are solely those of the author and do not necessarily reflect the views of the publisher, and the publisher hereby disclaims any responsibility for them.

Scripture taken from the Holy Bible, NEW INTERNATIONAL VERSION®. Copyright © 1973, 1978, 1984 by Biblica, Inc. All rights reserved worldwide. Used by permission. NEW INTERNATIONAL VERSION® and NIV® are registered trademarks of Biblica, Inc. Use of either trademark for the offering of goods or services requires the prior written consent of Biblica US, Inc.

ISBN: 978-1-5127-3520-8 (sc)
ISBN: 978-1-5127-3522-2 (hc)
ISBN: 978-1-5127-3521-5 (e)

Library of Congress Control Number: 2016904600

Print information available on the last page.

WestBow Press rev. date: 04/13/2016

Contents

Acknowledgements

Writing a book involves many individuals. I would like to thank the people who have helped to make this book possible.

Heather Rathnau and Dr. Connie Carson gave me excellent editorial advice. I must pay special recognition to Meagan Mason. She is the finest editor that a writer can have.

John E. Weis allowed my wife to take photographs of the spectacular instruments at the Steinway Piano Gallery in Paramus, New Jersey.

This book would not exist without all of the people whom I have described in these stories. These people have enhanced my life in many different ways.

A photograph of a worn out Bible is on the front cover of this book. This Bible belonged to my mother. She read this Bible every day. I will always be grateful for the many ways in which she influenced my life.

I want to thank WestBow Press for everything they did.

Finally, I want to thank my wife, Sondra Paulson, for her love and support. I also want to say that *Piano Moments* would not be complete without her beautiful photographs.

Endorsements

Piano Moments is an engaging devotional filled with short stories from the life of a Christian pianist. The skills taught through music study come alive in exciting life experiences—lessons on fear and grace, sacrifice and commitment, hard work and maturity, beauty and tranquility, not to mention donuts and Captain Silver, are intertwined with artistic, award-winning photographs and real-life applications. Musician or otherwise, take a moment and be blessed!
—Heather Rathnau, NCTM, Theory Time, Missouri City, Texas

Piano Moments offers refreshing, concise, and practical contemplations. It's a musical rendition of Our Daily Bread! Not written only for the musically adept, the book is an original compilation of photographs, stories, Bible verses, and practical questions that are relevant, thought-provoking, and inviting. It applies to the teacher, piano student, and music aficionado.

—Dr. Connie Carson, healthcare consultant

Piano Moments is a gem! Each story, filled with biblical wisdom, comes with appropriate Scriptures and thoughts for meditation. From "Never Too Old to Learn" to "Disagreeing with My Teacher," the topics are chosen with care and direction. Whether you are a pianist or not, you will be blessed by the spiritual nuggets found in *Piano Moments!*

—Dr. Patrick Kavanaugh, executive director
of the Christian Performing Artists' Fellowship

I can think of a hundred reasons for you to use Mark Paulson's new resource, *Piano Moments*. Here you will find a hundred nuggets of inspiration to energize your joy for music and faith. Inside the cover are a hundred well crafted moments of grace to prepare your heart for a more meaningful sharing of your life song! Let the music begin!

—Joseph Martin, director of Sacred Publications
at Hal Leonard/Shawnee Press

Introduction

Piano Moments is a collection of short stories that relate to the piano. The piano has played a significant role in my life ever since I was a child. Each person has special moments in their life that they will never be able to forget. These are some of the stories that I remember.

Each piano moment includes a Bible verse and life applications. Your life can become better if you will take the time to meditate on these reflections. While you are reading *Piano Moments*, try to remember stories in your life that are similar to the ones that I have shared. I encourage you to keep a journal while you read *Piano Moments*. Answer the questions at the end of each chapter and record your own memories, lessons, and favorite verses. You do not need to be a pianist to understand and benefit from these piano moments. I am sure that you will be able to identify with these stories in one way or another.

1. Parents

I grew up in a small town in Minnesota where my father owned a music store. He sold pianos, organs, and guitars. The store also offered music lessons. I spent many hours at the music studio while my grandfather looked after me. I did not know how to turn on the organs, so I played the pianos. There was a bakery near the store. I remember eating donuts on several occasions and being told to keep my sticky fingers off the piano keys. When I was five years old, I called my mother on the telephone and asked her if I could take piano lessons. She said that I could take lessons, but she insisted on sitting with me every day while I practiced. I wish I could say that I was an enthusiastic student, but that was not the case. My mother had to force me to practice. I enjoyed making up songs, but I did not like to play the music that was assigned. I asked to quit the lessons many times; fortunately, my mother never allowed that to happen.

> Start children off on the way they should go, and even when they are old they will not turn from it.
>
> —Proverbs 22:6

Parents play a significant role in their children's lives. What positive influences did your parents have on you? Try to remember your first childhood memories. What particular things come to your mind? How old were you when you first heard about God? What can you do to become a better parent?

2. Success

The music store where I took lessons had dozens of students. People took lessons on the organ, piano, guitar, and accordion. All of the students were required to play in recitals, which lasted for several hours. I gave my first public performance at one of those recitals. The room where I played was hot and smelly. I still remember the organ and accordion duets. I wish that I could forget them, but they are chiseled in my memory forever. My first performance was a success—even though it lasted less than a minute.

> He holds success in store for the upright; he is a shield
> to those whose walk is blameless.
>
> —Proverbs 2:7

Successful experiences shape our lives in many different ways. Early successes or failures can have a significant effect on our ability to function later on in life. What is the first memory that you have of being successful?

3. Be Prepared

I joined Cub Scouts when I was six years old. I did not know that I needed to memorize the Cub Scout Promise: "I promise to do my best to do my duty to God and my country, to help other people, and to obey the Law of the Pack." I was called up by myself, in front of all the other scouts, to recite the promise. I could not say a single word. All of the scouts laughed at me. The adult leader tried to help me, but it was very embarrassing. I never forgot that experience. I had recently played the piano in that same auditorium. Because of my humiliation when I was a Cub Scout, I always tried to prepare my students for their recitals well in advance. I never wanted any of my students to be unprepared for their performance.

> But in your hearts revere Christ as Lord. Always be prepared to give an answer to everyone who asks you to give the reason for the hope that you have. But do this with gentleness and respect.
>
> —1 Peter 3:15

We must always prepare for particular events. Avoiding embarrassing situations is important. Have you ever been unprepared? How have you treated other people who were not ready to perform?

4. Fearfully and Wonderfully Made

One October, when I was seven years old, my teacher assigned me a piece called "Captain Silver." I immediately told her that I was going to be Captain Silver for Halloween. I was excited to be that character. Being Captain Silver made me feel very special.

> I praise you because I am fearfully and wonderfully made; your works are wonderful; I know that full well.
>
> —Psalm 139:14

If you could dress up to be anyone, who would that person be? Why did you choose that individual? Some people wish that they could be a different person. They envy that person's life. It is important to remember that God has created you. He loves you just the way that you are. You do not need to be somebody else.

5. God's Plan for You

My grandfather watched me most of the time when I was growing up. He took me to the local tavern so that he could shoot pool and play cards with his friends. I heard many songs on the jukebox. I was able to play those songs by ear on the piano at the saloon. Eventually, I could play over fifty songs. By the time that I was eight years old, people in the tavern would give me money if I could play a song that they requested. I had no idea at the time that I had begun my performance career.

> "For I know the plans I have for you," declares the Lord, "plans to prosper you and not to harm you, plans to give you hope and a future."
>
> —Jeremiah 29:11

What is the first thing that inspired you to have the career that you are doing today? What are a few positive things that you enjoy about your current job? How does your job fit into God's plan for your life?

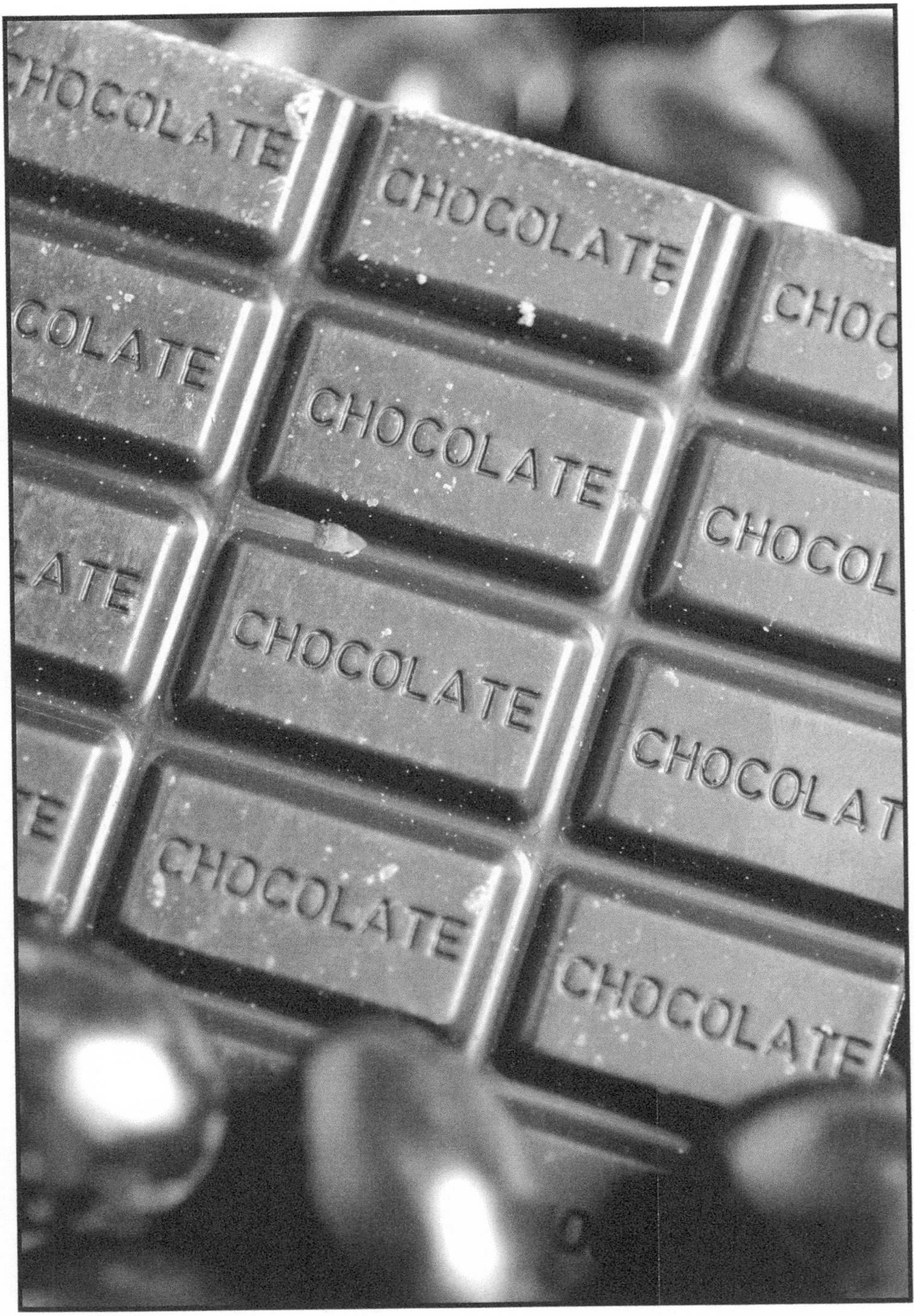
CHOCOLATE
CHOCOLATE
CHOCOLATE
CHOCOLATE
CHOCOLATE

6. Memorable Gifts

When I was eight years old, I had a paper route. I delivered thirteen newspapers every day. I had to collect money from my customers once a week. One man always gave me a Hershey's candy bar with his payment. I have not delivered papers for nearly fifty years, but I still remember that guy quite often when I eat a candy bar. I kept that man in mind when I taught my piano students. I never knew what I might do or say that could instill a memory that my students would not forget.

> Thanks be to God for his indescribable gift!
>
> —2 Corinthians 9:15

Try to recall a present that somebody gave to you that left a lasting memory. Why do you still remember that gift? Take a moment to meditate on the gifts that God has given to you. How do God's gifts remind you of Him?

7. Gray Hairs

When I was five years old, my mother started to go to a local nursing home to sing hymns for the residents. When I was nine years old, my father asked me to learn several songs. The pieces were from the thirties and forties. As an adult, I played those songs several times a week for residents in nursing homes. That was a wonderful way for me to earn extra money. Over the years, I played the piano in nursing homes more than nine hundred times.

> Even to your old age and gray hairs I am he, I am he who will sustain you. I have made you, and I will carry you; I will sustain you and I will rescue you.
>
> —Isaiah 46:4

Do you know an elderly person? Becoming old is something that most of us will experience. What are your thoughts about growing old?

8. Never Alone

I did not have many friends when I was a child. The only time that most people noticed me was when I played the piano. Without the piano, I would have been very lonely. People liked me because I played the piano. The piano brought people together. When I became an adult, I noticed that people would come to the piano whenever I played at parties—especially if they were alone. Some people liked to sing while I played their favorite songs. Other people came over to me just to have a conversation. I met many wonderful people that way. The piano made that possible.

> Be strong and courageous. Do not be afraid or terrified because of them, for the LORD your God goes with you; he will never leave you nor forsake you.
>
> —Deuteronomy 31:6

We all get lonely at different times in our lives. What are some of your favorite ways to meet new people? How do you deal with the times when you feel lonely? Have you ever asked God to be with you when you were lonely? Know that He is always present.

9. The Harvest

I took piano lessons from the time that I was five until I was twelve years old. When I turned twelve, my mother said that I could stop taking lessons from my teacher. I thought that I was done with lessons forever. That lasted for about a week. My mother informed me that I was going to meet a new teacher to see if I would like her better. I did not like that instructor at all. My mother informed me a month later that I was going to meet a different teacher. I did not like that person either. My mom introduced me to five more teachers during the next few months, but none of them were acceptable to me. I did not appreciate it at the time, but my mother did not want me to stop taking piano lessons.

> Let us not become weary in doing good, for at the proper time, we will reap a harvest if we do not give up.
>
> —Galatians 6:9

Try to recall a person who encouraged you to keep going when you wanted to stop doing something. Have you ever motivated somebody to continue what they were doing when they wanted to quit? Have you ever thought about giving up your faith? Always remember that God will never stop loving you.

10. God Is Watching

I liked to improvise music when I was a child. I would sit at the piano for hours creating melodies. Some of the songs were happy, and other songs were sad. My mother would smile when I played songs that were happy, but when I played sad songs, she would come over to the piano and give me a hug. My mom always knew how I felt whenever she heard me play the piano.

> You know when I sit and when I rise; you perceive my thoughts from afar.
>
> —Psalm 139:2

How are you feeling today? Why do you feel that way? God knows everything about you. He knows when you are happy and when you are sad. He knows your thoughts from afar, but He is always willing to give you a hug whenever you need one. Do you believe this?

11. Rules

My mother took me to a Baptist church every week. I heard hundreds of hymns at those services. I could play most of the songs by ear when I was twelve years old. The church had very strict rules. I was better than the pianist who played the hymns, but I was never allowed to play at that church because I refused to wear a tie. I am sure that if I wore a tie, people would have told me that my hair was too long.

> Since you died with Christ to the elemental spiritual forces of this world, why, as though you still belonged to the world, do you submit to its rules: "Do not handle! Do not taste! Do not touch!"? These rules, which have to do with things that are all destined to perish with use, are based on merely human commands and teachings. Such regulations indeed have an appearance of wisdom, with their self-imposed worship, their false humility and their harsh treatment of the body, but they lack any value in restraining sensual indulgence.
>
> —Colossians 2:20–23

Try to think of some rules or requirements that have kept you from sharing your talents with other people. Were those rules or requirements reasonable? There are times when rules will be necessary for you to follow, but you must never be afraid to say NO if somebody asks you to do something that is unacceptable. Is it easy or difficult for you to obey God's rules?

12. Teach Me

My father was an avid golfer. I stopped taking piano lessons when I was twelve years old so that I could play more golf with him. I had played golf every summer since I was eight years old, so I became very skilled. Some people wanted to learn how to play golf, so they asked me to give them lessons. During their first lesson, I proceeded to tell them more than twenty things that they needed to know. My instructions were very confusing, so they never wanted to play the game again. That was the first time that I gave somebody a lesson. I realized that I needed to keep my instructions simple so that my students could learn from me. Though I did not know it at the time, the golf course was where I started my training to become a full-time piano teacher.

Show me your ways, LORD, teach me your paths.

—Psalm 25:4

Try to recall the first time that you were a teacher. How did it go? Do you prefer being a teacher or a student? God wants to be your master. His instructions are clear and easy to understand. Are you willing to listen to Him?

13. Different Interests

Science was my worst subject in school. Other classmates loved to do experiments or look at things under a microscope. I was never interested. The science teacher told the class that everyone had to do a project for the upcoming science fair. Some of the students spent weeks preparing for that event. The time came to display the projects. The room was full of elaborate presentations. I wrote a song about pollution. I played the song on the piano and sang the words. It was an easy way for me to complete the required assignment. I received a good grade for my song even though it was quite different from the other projects. I was glad that the science fair was over. I never enjoyed anything about science. I assume that was one reason I became a piano teacher instead of an engineer.

> So Christ himself gave the apostles, the prophets, the evangelists, the pastors and teachers, to equip his people for works of service, so that the body of Christ may be built up until we all reach unity in the faith and in the knowledge of the Son of God and become mature, attaining to the whole measure of the fullness of Christ.
>
> —Ephesians 4:11–13

What was your favorite subject in school? What was your least favorite subject? What other careers would you enjoy if you were not doing what you do today? Everyone has different interests. We all do different things, but everyone has a purpose. How can you use your talents and skills to serve God?

14. Wasted Time

I did not use my time wisely on the piano when I was a child. Other piano students spent endless hours refining their skills. By the time that they were in high school, they were able to play very well. I did not take my lessons seriously. I never practiced my assignments. I was able to play many songs by ear, but there were other things that I did not learn. I cannot go back to use my time in a more efficient way.

> Teach us to number our days that we may gain a heart of wisdom.

> —Psalm 90:12

We have all wasted lots of time in our lives. We cannot go back in time, but we can make the days ahead more productive. What are some ways in which you have wasted time in your life? How can you use your time more wisely in the future? Do you include God in your daily activities?

15. Changing Directions

When I was seventeen years old, I wanted to study music in college. Unfortunately, I discovered that there were many prerequisites and skills that I needed to have. I could play hundreds of songs by ear, but that was not good enough. I had to know scales, chords, theory, and other things. I had tickets to hear Van Cliburn, but instead, I decided to go to a piano master class. Lazar Berman, who was a famous pianist, was the presenter. I was amazed at the proficiency of the participants. I realized that I had to make many improvements in my playing if I were ever going to get into a music school. I met a wonderful piano teacher at the master class. That teacher would eventually play a significant role in my music career and my life. I gave up tickets to hear Van Cliburn, but the time that I spent at the master class was more valuable.

> Create in me a pure heart, O God, and renew a steadfast spirit within me.
>
> —Psalm 51:10

Has there ever been a time when you had to make some significant improvements in your life? What did you have to change? What are some changes that you can make today? Have you ever asked God to help you make those changes?

16. Serious Study

When I was seventeen years old, I went to the home of the piano teacher that I met at the Lazar Berman master class. She lived on a farm that was twelve miles away from where I lived. I needed that teacher to teach me the skills that were necessary to get into college. We set up a plan to reach that goal. I would practice for six hours every day and go to her home twice a week for lessons. It was not possible for me to learn everything in a short amount of time, so I had to take lessons with her for one year. During that period, the teacher also showed me how I could have a serious relationship with God.

> Do your best to present yourself to God as one approved, a worker who does not need to be ashamed and who correctly handles the word of truth.
>
> —2 Timothy 2:15

Try to remember a time in your life when you were a full-time student. Did you enjoy doing the work that you were assigned? How do you currently use the things that you learned when you were a student? Do you ever study the Bible? Do you have a close relationship with God?

17. Acceptance

I received a letter in the mail. A college accepted me into their music program. That was quite an accomplishment because I could not meet their requirements a year earlier. Receiving that college acceptance letter was an important moment in my life. It indicated that a school believed that I was ready to meet their challenges. I was happy to know that a college wanted me.

> All those the Father gives me will come to me, and whoever comes to me I will never drive away.
>
> —John 6:37

Where did you go to college? Was college important in your life? Most people have to work very hard to get accepted into a college. You can always come to God. He will never turn you away.

18. Ears to Hear

My piano teacher and I drove over one hundred miles to hear Rudolf Serkin play the piano. Mr. Serkin was one of the finest pianists in the world. Just before the recital was about to begin, we were told that John Browning was going to perform instead of Mr. Serkin. I had never heard of John Browning, even though he was a famous pianist. I was very disappointed. Instead of enjoying Mr. Browning's recital, I refused to listen to him. I was present in the auditorium, but I closed my ears. John Browning gave a beautiful concert, but I did not hear it.

> Then Jesus said, "Whoever has ears to hear, let them hear."
>
> —Mark 4:9

Have you ever refused to listen to somebody because you believed that your opinion was the only one that mattered? Are you usually interested in what other people have to say? Do you think about what you are going to say while people are talking to you? What can you do to become a better listener? Do you prefer to listen to God or to tell Him what is on your mind? How does God speak to you?

19. A Jealous God

One of the most memorable moments in my life occurred when my mother, my piano teacher, and I attended a piano recital that was presented by Vladimir Horowitz. We arrived at the concert hall in my piano teacher's farm truck. People stared at us when we drove up in that strange looking vehicle. I was simply thrilled to be there. I remember seeing Mr. Horowitz walk out on the stage wearing his bow tie. I felt like I was in the presence of royalty. The playing was better than anything that I had ever heard. I was inspired, but I also recognized that I was never going to become a concert pianist. All I could do was enjoy the music that Mr. Horowitz had to offer. We rode back home in the farm truck knowing that we had probably heard the greatest pianist in the world.

> Do not worship any other god, for the LORD, whose name is Jealous, is a jealous God.
>
> —Exodus 34:14

Who is your favorite celebrity? Have you ever been jealous of that person? Some people receive a significant amount of attention because of their wealth, their beauty, or their talents. God is a jealous God. You can admire other people for their accomplishments, but God wants you to give your total worship and praise to Him.

20. Never Too Old to Learn

My mother started to take piano lessons with my piano teacher when she was fifty-eight years old. She knew how to play hymns and a few other simple songs, but she decided that she wanted to learn how to play classical music. Vladimir Horowitz had inspired her to study the piano again after she heard him perform in a recital. I shared my piano with her because she needed to practice. Her lessons continued off and on throughout her life. Eventually, my mother made a recording of her playing when she was ninety years old. She even gave a solo piano recital. I realized from her that nobody is ever too old to learn something that is new.

> Therefore, we do not lose heart. Though outwardly we are wasting away, yet inwardly we are being renewed day by day.
>
> —2 Corinthians 4:16

What is something that you have always wanted to learn? It is never too late to learn something new. God wants you to know more about Him. He desires to renew you inwardly every day. Will you allow Him to do this?

21. Knowing Where to Go

I thought that I was going to a recital with my piano teacher. My piano teacher was instead going to surprise me with an opera performance. She thought that she had purchased opera tickets for *The Merry Widow*. We ended up seeing the *Dialogues of the Carmelites*. That was the first time that I ever went to an opera. The opera was in French. I was not prepared to see the nuns get their heads chopped off at the end of the story. The opera was a unique experience. It was good to experience that kind of music, but I wished that I had known where I was going.

> I will instruct you and teach you in the way you should go; I will counsel you with my eye upon you.
>
> —Psalm 32:8

Have you ever had to ask somebody for directions? Have you ever been confused or unsure of where you should go? How did that make you feel? What can you do to avoid those situations in the future? Do you ever ask God to tell you where He wants you to go?

22. God Knows Everything

My first semester in college was very challenging. My piano teacher had prepared me for the music requirements, but I was not ready for many of the academic assignments. I should have worked harder in high school. I had never written a term paper. I asked the professor to explain how to write a term paper during his class. The entire class laughed at me. They acted as if they knew everything. I have always believed that it is important to be sensitive whenever a person does not know something and to guide them in ways that will make the learning experience more enjoyable. I tried to do that for all of my piano students.

> He determines the number of the stars and calls them each by name. Great is our Lord and mighty in power; his understanding has no limit.
>
> —Psalm 147:4–5

Have you ever helped a person learn something that was common knowledge to other individuals? Were you able to teach that person in a way that was supportive and encouraging? Nobody has all of the answers except God. God has all the answers, and you can go to Him at any time. He will never laugh at you.

23. A Kind Word

When I was in college, I performed in a large auditorium for the first time. I played the *Prelude* from the *English Suite No. 3 in G Minor* by Johann Sebastian Bach. I was extremely nervous. I began to play the piece, but it quickly fell apart. I started over again. I made mistakes in the same place. I sat on the stage in complete silence for over a minute. I was terrified. I tried one more time. That time I managed to get through the entire piece. I felt ashamed and discouraged. I received a card in the mail the following day from a lady who attended the recital. She told me that there were several things that she liked about my playing. That encouragement was very helpful to me. Her letter inspired me to work harder so that I could play better the next time.

> Anxiety weighs down the heart, but a kind word cheers it up.
>
> —Proverbs 12:25

Try to remember an experience in your life that did not go well. What have you done to avoid repeating an experience like that in the future? Have you ever offered encouragement to someone when things did not go well for them? God wants us to encourage one another. Who are you able to inspire today?

24. Learning Something New

My father sold pianos and organs when I was young. I could never find the power switch, so I did not learn how to play the organ. I only played the piano. I played hymns on a piano every Sunday while I was in college. Over the years, I played the piano in several different churches. It might have opened up many more opportunities for me if I had learned how to turn the organs on when I was younger.

> Instruct the wise and they will be wiser still; teach the righteous and they will add to their learning.

> —Proverbs 9:9

What is one thing that you would like to be able to do that you cannot do today? What has prohibited you from learning something new? Is there something that God wants to teach you?

25. Accepting Criticism

Shortly after I had completed my first year of college in Minnesota, I met one of the finest piano teachers in the world. She came from New Jersey to adjudicate several piano students and to give a master class. That teacher had studied at the Juilliard School. I was able to have a piano lesson with her at the end of her busy day. She was exhausted. Every wrong note that I played made her angry. When the lesson was over, she told me to choose a different major in college instead of music. I was very discouraged, but I was not going to give up my dreams. I attended church the following day after I had that lesson. I sat next to a visitor who was driving out east that afternoon. I asked if I could ride with her to New Jersey. She said yes. I contacted the piano teacher from New Jersey to see if I could study with her. She reluctantly said that she would teach me. I left that afternoon. I arrived at my new teacher's home four days later with three dollars and some music. A new chapter in my life was about to begin.

> Whoever loves discipline loves knowledge, but he who hates reproof is stupid.
>
> —Proverbs 12:1

Has anyone ever been critical about something that you did? That may have been discouraging, but it also might have helped you to become a better person. Be willing to accept advice if it can enhance the things that you are doing. That information might change your life forever. What advice has God given to you?

26. Helping Others

When I moved to New Jersey, I did not know where to live or how to support myself. Several piano teachers took turns caring for me in various ways even though they had just met me. Those teachers made sure that I had everything that I needed. They also taught me to help anyone who needed my assistance. Those teachers did not ever give me piano lessons, but I learned a greater lesson from them. They taught me that piano teachers help other people whenever they are able.

> John answered, "Anyone who has two shirts should share with the one who has none, and anyone who has food should do the same."
>
> —Luke 3:11

Try to remember someone who helped you in a special way. How did that make you feel? How have you helped another person? God wants you to come to Him whenever you have a need.

27. Assistance

My piano teacher from New Jersey allowed me to live in her home for two months. She gave me food and a place to sleep. I did chores for her in exchange for my lessons. I needed money, so she taught me how to teach other students. My teacher helped me buy a bicycle so that I could go from one house to another giving piano lessons. Sometimes I had to ride my bicycle to my students' homes in the rain or the snow on busy highways. I was not a very skilled teacher in the beginning, but my teacher helped me to become better.

> And my God will meet all your needs according to the riches of his glory in Christ Jesus.
>
> —Philippians 4:19

Everyone needs help from other people at various times in their life. Nobody makes it in this world on their own. How has somebody helped you? What can you do to help another person? How does God supply your needs?

28. Breaking Bread

I always taught my students in their homes. When I started my teaching career, I did not have much money. Many of the families gave me meals. Having dinner with my students was a regular part of my teaching schedule. My students were like family to me. Eating with my students allowed me to get to know them in a personal way. Teaching music was only one reason I met with my students and their families every week—we were also friends. The relationship that I had with my students was very personal.

> They devoted themselves to the apostles' teaching and
> to fellowship, to the breaking of bread and to prayer.
>
> —Acts 2:42

Having a meal with another person is a good way to get to know them better. Some people schedule weekly lunch dates to develop better relationships. When was the last time that you had lunch or dinner with an individual to get to know them better? Take somebody out for a meal very soon.

29. Lost Sheep

I traveled on a bicycle for the first year when I moved to New Jersey. One day I came to a fork in the road. I needed to decide if I should go left or right. I went left. That decision took me ten miles on a busy highway in the wrong direction. I did not know where I was. I called my piano teacher. She was able to tell me how I could get to her home. I was happy to see her when I arrived.

> Suppose one of you has a hundred sheep and loses one of them. Doesn't he leave the ninety-nine in the open country and go after the lost sheep until he finds it? And when he finds it, he joyfully puts it on his shoulders and goes home. Then he calls his friends and neighbors together and says, "Rejoice with me; I have found my lost sheep."
>
> —Luke 15:4–6

We all make wrong turns in life. Try to recall a wrong turn that you've made. How did you find your way back home? Attempt to help somebody who has lost their way.

30. Praise Him with Strings

I rode my bicycle past a large church in New Jersey. The following Sunday I attended the worship service at that church. A man in the congregation introduced me to the organist. She told me about a local Bible college, where she was the head of the music department. I played a few different styles of music for her. She said that I could continue to study with my current piano teacher and receive a music scholarship if I came to the school. I applied to that Bible college the next day and was accepted.

> Praise him with timbrel and dancing, praise him with the strings and pipe.
>
> —Psalm 150:4

There are many different kinds of music. What types of music do you prefer? Does music help you to worship God? Do you believe that all music is appropriate for worshiping Him?

31. One Language

I was the accompanist for the college choir. We presented concerts in many different churches throughout the United States. The director's ancestors were Norwegian, so she took the choir on a tour to Norway. My ancestors were also Norwegian, so that made the trip extra special for me. All of the pastors gave their sermons in Norwegian. I could not understand a word that they were saying. But everyone enjoyed the music that the choir sang. I learned that people can appreciate music the same way in different parts of the world.

> Now the whole world had one language and a common speech.

> —Genesis 11:1

The Bible says that there was a time when the world had one language. Try to imagine what that would be like today. Can you speak any other languages? What other languages would you like to learn? How does God talk to you?

32. Sacrifices

I moved away from my biological family in 1979. My father passed away in 1980. I was never with him during the time when he was sick. I wish that I could have been with my dad for his last days, but that was not possible. My brother passed away a few years later. I was not with him when he was ill either. Over the years, I had to be away from several family events, including the funerals of two of my grandparents. Some of those sacrifices were choices that I would not make today. Other sacrifices were necessary. Sacrifices are never easy to make, but every person has encountered them at one time or another.

> And everyone who has left houses or brothers or sisters or father or mother or wife or children or fields for my sake will receive a hundred times as much and will inherit eternal life.
>
> —Matthew 19:29

What are some of the most significant sacrifices that you have made in your life? Would you make those sacrifices again if you could go back in time? Has God ever asked you to sacrifice something? Were you willing to make that sacrifice for Him?

33. Hope for Tomorrow

My father died in 1980, and my brother in 1984. I played the piano for their funerals. Playing the piano at those funerals gave me comfort in a particular way. The piano also allowed me to offer support to friends and family members. That was a sad time for me, but I knew that I would see my father and my brother again.

> Brothers and sisters, we do not want you to be uninformed about those who sleep in death so that you do not grieve like the rest of mankind, who have no hope. For we believe that Jesus died and rose again, and so we believe that God will bring with Jesus those who have fallen asleep in him.
>
> —1 Thessalonians 4:13–14

Losing a family member is one of the most difficult things that a person can ever experience. Try to recall some of your fondest memories of a loved one who has passed away. Do you believe that you will see them again someday? The Bible says that you will.

34. Children

Charlie was my first talented piano student. After a few months of lessons, he was playing music that would take other students a couple of years to learn. Then my piano teacher met Charlie. She did not believe that I was experienced enough to teach him, so Charlie became her student. Charlie began to win local piano competitions. Winning piano competitions was good for Charlie's self-esteem. Everything was going well for him. Unfortunately, Charlie was killed one night in an automobile accident when he was returning home from his piano lesson. Everyone was devastated. Nobody ever knows when their time in this world will come to an end. It can be over at any moment. Charlie was a remarkable individual.

> Jesus said, "Let the little children come to me, and do not hinder them, for the kingdom of heaven belongs to such as these."
>
> —Matthew 19:14

God loves children. They are very precious to Him. Try to think of a child that you know. Give that child a hug or do something nice for that person today.

35. Many Rooms

I needed to find a place to live that was away from my college, and one of the other students at the school needed a roommate. I made an appointment to meet with his eighty-five-year-old landlady. I did not fully appreciate her house when I first entered the living room. I told the lady that her home might meet my needs. The woman looked me in the eye and said that she had a spectacular house and that I'd better never forget it. Her house was lovely, and the price was right, so I moved in that afternoon. The next morning, she brought me coffee on a silver platter at 6:00 a.m. When she saw my messy room, she scolded me and told me to hang up my clothes. She had a grand piano in the center of her living room. She said that she expected to hear me practice on it every day. All of that happened during the first twenty-four hours that I lived in her home. She continued bringing me coffee every morning while I was living there. I did not know that she was going to transform my life in the years to come.

> My Father's house has many rooms; if that were not so, would I have told you that I am going there to prepare a place for you? And if I go and prepare a place for you, I will come back and take you to be with me that you also may be where I am.
>
> —John 14:2–3

Try to picture heaven in your mind. Imagine all of the rooms. What other things do you see? Are you looking forward to living with God in heaven someday?

36. Time

I enjoyed playing the piano at Christmas parties. While I was going to college, I was hired to play at a party from seven o'clock to eleven o'clock. At eleven o'clock, I was asked to stay until the party was over. The party did not end until nine o'clock the next morning. I took many breaks. I received the biggest performance check in my life and my employers even added a tip. It was a very merry Christmas for me that year.

> But do not forget this one thing, dear friends: With the Lord a day is like a thousand years, and a thousand years are like a day.

> —2 Peter 3:8

Everyone has a schedule. How does the clock play a role in your life? Can you think of some examples when watching the clock should not be significant to you? When is it necessary for you to be on time? How is God's time different from yours?

37. Test Me

I was hired to play Christmas carols at the Irish Embassy in New York City. That was going to be a very special event, so I needed to be on time. There was a blizzard in the forecast, so I decided to go into the city early in the morning. I only lived an hour away from the embassy, but the driving conditions started to get difficult. Within a matter of minutes, the roads were covered with snow. Cars were not moving at all. Hours went by as I struggled to get into the city. The snow continued to fall, but the traffic finally started to move forward. I arrived in the city, but I was still a long way away from the embassy. I reached my destination only a few minutes before I was scheduled to perform. It had taken nine hours to travel twelve miles. The people were happy that I was there. I was obligated to fulfill my commitment.

> Test me, Lord, and try me, examine my heart and my mind; for I have always been mindful of your unfailing love and have lived in reliance on your faithfulness.

> —Psalm 26:2–3

It is important to fulfill your responsibilities whenever people depend on you. What have you done to demonstrate that you are a responsible person? How can you become more dependable? Can you think of a time when God showed his faithfulness to you?

38. God's Children

I took a job as the director of children's music at an Episcopal church. The church had a special service just for the children and their parents. The boys and girls wore red robes, so we called them the Red Hots. Occasionally they would sing in the adult service. Most of the children were about five years of age, so all of the hymns were simple to sing. The children collected the offering and read Bible verses. That was a place where children and busy parents could offer their praises to God in a special way.

> Through the praise of children and infants you have established a stronghold against your enemies, to silence the foe and the avenger.
>
> —Psalm 8:2

Every parent desires to be loved by their children. That is one of the greatest things that a parent can ever receive. God also wants to be loved by His children. Do you consider yourself to be one of God's children? How do you show your love to Him?

39. Priceless Love

My landlady transformed my life in many different ways. She exposed me to great literature. We stayed up late at night to discuss religion, philosophy, and politics. One night we stayed up until 4:00 a.m. to listen to a thunderstorm. That woman was never afraid to tell me anything if it could improve my life in a significant way. She loved to hear classical music. We occasionally went to concerts together. One day I said to her that I could not afford to stay in her home. Students were not signing up for piano lessons. I was charging five dollars for a thirty-minute lesson. My landlady told me that I was living in an area where people determined a person's talents and skills by the fees that they charged. She said that I would get more students if I doubled my rates. I changed my rates to ten dollars for thirty minutes. Within a short amount of time, several people signed up for lessons. A year later my landlady asked me to double my rates again. More people began to tell their friends about me. The following year she encouraged me to increase my rates one last time. My studio was full, and I had a waiting list. I was able to have a successful business for many years after that because I listened to the advice from my landlady.

> Jesus answered, "If you want to be perfect, go, sell your possessions and give to the poor, and you will have treasure in heaven. Then come, follow me."

> —Matthew 19:21

People often have a greater appreciation for something if it is expensive. You deserve to be paid fairly for the work that you do. What is the most valuable gift that you have ever purchased for yourself or someone else? What are a few things that you possess that money cannot buy? God's love is free. It is priceless, but He wants to give it to you.

40. Finish the Race

I witnessed incredible determination at my studio's first student recital. A young boy performed "The Entertainer" by Scott Joplin. The boy played most of the notes correctly, but when he came to the last line, everything fell apart. He struggled at the end, so he began to play the entire piece over. He had difficulty in the same spot, so he started again for the third time. When he came near the end, he played every note very slowly. He was determined to get through those last four measures. It took forever. He eventually came to the final chord and played it perfectly. The entire audience rose to their feet with great enthusiasm and gave him a standing ovation.

> I have fought the good fight, I have finished the race,
> I have kept the faith.
>
> —2 Timothy 4:7

Life is full of trials and difficulties. Everyone encounters some mistakes or hindrances along the way. The important thing is to persevere so that you can finish what you have started. Do not be discouraged if your life is not always easy. Strive to accomplish your goals. Try to recall some of the difficulties that you have faced in your life. How have you been able to overcome them? Can you remember a time when God helped you with a challenging situation?

41. Come as You Are

A student could not be on time for the spring piano recital because he had to play at a baseball game. The boy went to the event and scored the winning run by sliding into home plate. The family realized that they could still attend the recital, so they drove immediately to the church. The final performer was finishing her piece when the boy came into the room. He was wearing his messy baseball uniform. All of the other performers were wearing their best clothing. The boy's mother did not know if he would be allowed to play in the clothes that he was wearing. I told the student that it was his turn to perform. He played "Take Me Out to the Ball Game." Everyone was delighted that he was able to participate. It was a perfect way to end the recital. He tipped his cap to the audience.

> For he chose us in him before the creation of the world to be holy and blameless in his sight. In love, he predestined us for adoption to sonship through Jesus Christ, in accordance with his pleasure and will—to the praise of his glorious grace, which he has freely given us in the One he loves. In him, we have redemption through his blood, the forgiveness of sins, in accordance with the riches of God's grace.
>
> —Ephesians 1:4–7

Some people assume that they have to dress or act a certain way to be accepted. They think that they need a title or an important job to be respected. That can be very discouraging. Has anyone ever made you feel inadequate? Do not let that bother you. God has made you and accepted you for who you are.

42. Music Therapy

I transferred to a state college where I majored in music therapy. I was interested in studying music and psychology. One of my assignments was to play the piano for residents in several nursing homes. I also worked with mentally challenged children and people who had autism. It was incredible to see the different ways in which music could make their lives better. I eventually changed my major to piano performance, but I was grateful for what I learned in my music therapy classes.

> Now the Spirit of the Lord had departed from Saul, and an evil spirit from the Lord tormented him. Saul's attendants said to him, "See, an evil spirit from God is tormenting you. Let our lord command his servants here to search for someone who can play the lyre. He will play when the evil spirit from God comes on you, and you will feel better."
>
> —1 Samuel 16:14–16

Does music help you to feel better? What kinds of music do you enjoy? Are there songs that have a special meaning for you? What is a song that has had a significant impact on your life?

43. Knock on the Door

Most of my college teachers kept a professional relationship with all of their students. They did not talk to their students outside of the classroom. It was very lonely being in a practice room for several hours. There was a tuba professor who occasionally knocked on my practice room door to tell me that he enjoyed my playing. That teacher would say that I was getting better and that I should keep practicing. He usually only stayed for a minute, but I was grateful that he appreciated the work that I was doing.

> Here I am! I stand at the door and knock. If anyone hears my voice and opens the door, I will come in and eat with that person, and they with me.
>
> —Revelation 3:20

Have you ever knocked on somebody's door just to visit with them? How can you encourage someone today by knocking on their door? Have you ever heard God knocking on your door?

44. A New Song

When I was in college, I wrote many songs. One day I wrote a love song. I showed it to a friend of mine. She immediately thought that I had written the song for her. She was very excited. The next day she came into my practice room to talk about different ways in which we could enhance our relationship. I had to tell her that the song was for somebody else.

> He put a new song in my mouth, a hymn of praise to our God. Many will see and fear the LORD and put their trust in him.
>
> —Psalm 40:3

What is your favorite love song? Why does that song have a special meaning for you? Do you have a favorite hymn? Do you enjoy using music to tell God that you love Him?

45. Favoritism

I had to do some research at the Lincoln Center Library in New York City for a music history class. I spent the entire day looking at music manuscripts. The library was closing so I walked over to the Metropolitan Opera House. The opera was just about to begin. All of the people wore their finest clothes. I wore shorts and a tee shirt. A man had a ticket that he could not use, so he gave it to me for free. People in the audience were annoyed when I took my seat. They did not want to sit next to me. My ticket was very expensive. For a few hours, I was able to experience the same things that only rich people could afford.

> My brothers and sisters, believers in our glorious Lord Jesus Christ must not show favoritism.
>
> —James 2:1

Have you ever believed that you were less important than other people? Why did you think that those people were more special than you? Have you ever considered yourself to be more significant than another person? All people are equal in God's eyes.

46. Disagreeing with My Teacher

My piano teacher was giving a master class for her students. I was playing a piece composed by Beethoven. She told me that the piece needed to go faster. I told her that I preferred a slower tempo. My teacher immediately told me that I needed to follow her instructions. I was not willing to listen to her. That caused a problem in our relationship until I learned to be more obedient.

> The student is not above the teacher, nor a servant above his master.

> —Matthew 10:24

What is the best advice that anyone has ever given to you? Were you willing to apply that information to your life? What can you do to become more willing to follow the suggestions that other people offer?

47. Challenges

My piano teacher usually gave me music that was too difficult for me to play. I practiced for several hours every day, but I was never able to play the pieces very well. Over the years, I tried to find music for my students that they could master. It was important to challenge my students, but I never wanted them to feel discouraged.

> Take my yoke upon you and learn from me, for I am gentle and humble in heart, and you will find rest for your souls. For my yoke is easy and my burden is light.
>
> —Matthew 11:29–30

Do you ever get overwhelmed with difficult challenges? Are you able to accomplish most of the challenges that you face? Are there bigger challenges that you want to attempt? What are those challenges? How can God help you to fulfill those goals?

48. The Light of the World

I was hired to play at an outdoor party one evening from seven o'clock to eleven o'clock. I practiced everything that I was going to perform. I set up everything early to make sure that my equipment was working properly. I had fasteners for my music in case it was windy. All of my music was in order. Everything was going perfectly for the first two hours. People were coming up to thank me for the lovely music. Unfortunately, at nine o'clock, the sun went down. I forgot to bring a light. I had to play for the following two hours in complete darkness. I had played many other times without music, so I was able to continue. However, I was not able to play the music that people had requested.

> When Jesus spoke again to the people, he said, "I am the light of the world. Whoever follows me will never walk in darkness, but will have the light of life."
>
> —John 8:12

Have you ever taken the time to be grateful for your eyes and your ability to see the things that are around you? What are some things that you have taken for granted? Look around where you are and give thanks to God for everything that you can see.

49. Forgiveness

I was hired to accompany a twelve-year-old violinist. She was a remarkable performer. My part was easy, but her part was very challenging. Halfway through the piece, the girl played a couple of wrong notes. I do not believe anyone in the audience realized it except for her parents. The parents came backstage after the performance and told the girl that her entire performance was completely unacceptable. The parents were furious. They grabbed the girl's arm and immediately drove her home without attending the reception.

> I, even I, am he who blots out your transgressions,
> for my own sake and remembers your sins no more.
>
> —Isaiah 43:25

How do you react to people who do not meet your expectations? Are you willing to tolerate their mistakes and encourage them to do better the next time or do you demand perfection? How would you want to be treated by another person if you did something wrong? How does God want you to treat other people?

50. Buried Shoes

I taught piano lessons in my students' homes for most of my adult life. I always took off my shoes whenever I entered a person's home. One day I could not find my shoes at the end of a lesson. The entire family searched everywhere, but nobody could locate them. Finally, the mother decided to look in the backyard. She knew that their dog liked to bury things. In a few minutes, she came back with my shoes. The dog hid them next to the swimming pool.

> Nothing in all creation is hidden from God's sight.
> Everything is uncovered and laid bare before the eyes
> of him to whom we must give account.
>
> —Hebrews 4:13

Have you ever lost something that was very precious? Try to recall the anxious feelings that you had as you searched for the item that was missing. It is comforting to know that God never loses anything. He always knows where everything is.

51. *Practice*

I attended classes every day at my college in the morning and the early afternoon. I gave piano lessons for the rest of the day. I usually arrived back at the college around 9:30 at night. They locked the doors at ten o'clock, so I had to hide in a practice room until everyone had left. I was able to practice for three hours if I could stay awake. Hiding in a practice room was not fun, but that was the only way that I could prepare for my lessons and my performances.

> Whatever you have learned or received or heard from me, or seen in me—put it into practice. And the God of peace will be with you.

> —Philippians 4:9

Do you have goals that you are seeking to accomplish? What are those goals? How do you set aside time so that you can focus your attention on those objectives? Why are those goals important to you?

52. Brief Moments

My landlady loved to give parties. I attended a Christmas party that she gave at her home. I was a guest, but I also played Christmas songs on the piano. Just before the party was over, everyone was called into the living room to gather around the Christmas tree. I will never forget what happened next. The Christmas tree had real candles on it. My landlady always lit candles on her Christmas trees ever since she was a child. The lights were turned off, and we sang "Silent Night." Then my landlady said some kind words about her late husband. The entire event lasted less than two minutes. It is impossible to describe that special Christmas moment adequately. The event did not take long, but the memory will last until I die.

> For his anger lasts only a moment, but his favor lasts a lifetime; weeping may stay for the night, but rejoicing comes in the morning.
>
> —Psalm 30:5

Many experiences in life only last for a short amount of time. Some of those moments are happy, and some of them are sad. Try to recall a particular moment that did not last long, but that you can still remember. What could be the reason God wanted you to have that experience?

53. Humility

I was playing the piano in a person's home for a birthday party. A man came up to me and asked if he could sing a couple of songs from *Les Misérables*. Most of the people were in another room getting their dessert, so it was fun to have some company. I noticed that he was wearing a gold baseball ring with several diamonds. I asked him if he was a famous baseball player. He told me that he was once the bat boy on a championship baseball team. He sang his songs and then he went to join the other guests in the dining room. Later that night I found out that the man was never a bat boy. The man was the owner of that baseball team. I was impressed with his humility.

> Do nothing out of selfish ambition or vain conceit. Rather, in humility value others above yourselves.
>
> —Philippians 2:3

Would you like to be famous and receive praises from thousands of people? Do you seek admiration and respect from other individuals? Who are your greatest admirers? Can you give an example of a time when you displayed humility to another person? Jesus humbled himself for you when He died on the cross.

54. Home

I made a huge mistake one day. I moved away from where I was living. I loved my room and my landlady, but I found a different place to live that had a Steinway grand piano. The owner of the house told me that I could use it at any time. Eventually, she became jealous whenever I played the piano. She was also a pianist. I did not get to use it very often, and I missed my former landlady. One day, while I was visiting her, she told me that my old room was available. I told her that I would move back that afternoon, but I had to go home to get my possessions. She grabbed my arm and said, "YOU ARE HOME." I never forgot those words. Her house was my home. It was a very special place.

> My soul yearns, even faints, for the courts of the Lord;
> my heart and my flesh cry out for the living God.
> Even the sparrow has found a home, and the swallow
> a nest for herself, where she may have her young—a
> place near your altar, Lord Almighty, my King and
> my God. Blessed are those who dwell in your house;
> they are ever praising you.
>
> —Psalm 84:2–4

What makes your home unique? Would you like to live somewhere else? Where would that be? Are you residing in the place where God wants you to be right now?

55. Accomplishments

I attended college for six years. I kept changing colleges and my major, so it took longer than normal for me to graduate. I eventually earned an associate's degree in religious arts and a bachelor's degree in piano performance. My mother and my landlady were very proud of me. I would have never finished all of the requirements that were necessary to graduate without their support and encouragement.

> In all my prayers for all of you, I always pray with joy because of your partnership in the gospel from the first day until now, being confident of this, that he who began a good work in you will carry it on to completion until the day of Christ Jesus.
>
> —Philippians 1:4–6

What has been your greatest accomplishment? Was it easy or difficult to achieve? What new goals do you hope to accomplish in the future?

56. Work with All Your Heart

Shortly after I graduated from college, I was going to ask a girl if she would like to go on a date with me. We had not seen each other in over four years. Just before I was going to ask my question, the girl asked me if I was still a piano teacher or if I had found a real job. She did not understand that piano teaching is one of the best jobs that a person can ever have. There were many different careers that I could have chosen. I opted to be a piano teacher. I never asked that girl for a date.

> Whatever you do, work at it with all your heart, as working for the Lord, not for human masters.

> —Colossians 3:23

Why did you choose the career that you currently have? Give some reasons why your job is important to you. What can you do to make your job more meaningful? Do you strive to do your work with all your heart?

and weaves her own cloth.

She welcomes the poor.

She helps the needy.

She does not worry about

it snows.

They all have fine

warm.

PROV

57. Finding a Wife

I purchased two tickets to a guitar recital. John Williams was the performer. I wanted to take a particular girl, but she was not interested in going. I took a conducting class at a college just for fun after I earned my piano performance degree. I asked a girl in the class if she would like to go with me to the recital. She said yes. We continued to date for several months. One day I told her that I had spent all of my money on something that was very special. She was eager to see what I had bought. I brought her to my apartment so that she could see my new piano. She was not excited about my purchase at all. She thought that I had bought something else. A couple of months later I gave her the engagement ring that she wanted.

> A wife of noble character who can find? She is worth far more than rubies. Her husband has full confidence in her and lacks nothing of value.
>
> —Proverbs 31:10–11

Choosing a partner is one of the most important decisions that a person ever makes. What are the most important qualities that you desire in a spouse? What are your best qualities that you can offer to that other person? How can God help you to become a better person for your partner?

58. The Announcement

I usually asked my landlady for advice about everything. I did not consult her regarding one of the most significant decisions that I ever made in my life. I gave a party at my landlady's home. I invited all of my friends. I played the piano and spent time with everyone. Just before the night was over, I called my friends into the living room so that I could make an important announcement. I told everyone that I was getting married. Everyone was happy except for my landlady. She stood quietly in a corner. She realized that I would be moving away and living with another person. I should have informed my landlady in advance about my decision, but it was too difficult for me to tell her.

> But at the beginning of creation, God "made them male and female." "For this reason, a man will leave his father and mother and be united to his wife, and the two will become one flesh." So they are no longer two, but one flesh.

> —Mark 10:6–8

What is the most important announcement that you have ever made? Did you ask advice from anyone before you said it? When was the first time that you were away from your family for more than a month? How difficult was that separation for you?

59. Treasures

My wife and I lived in a small apartment after we got married. One day I went to a garage sale where a man was selling a Bechstein grand piano for a very reasonable price. He did not know anything about the piano. Bechstein pianos are spectacular instruments. I purchased the piano, but I did not have a place to keep it. Another piano teacher was willing to put the Bechstein in her home. My wife and I realized that we needed a bigger apartment. We were able to find a larger apartment on the second floor of a house. I was excited that I was going to be able to have my Bechstein where I lived. Unfortunately, we found out when the movers arrived that the piano was too large to go up the stairs. The owner of the house assessed the problem and decided to cut a large opening in the entryway with a chainsaw so that the piano would fit. That act of kindness made it possible for me to have my grand piano in the living room. The new apartment also gave us more room to store all of our other possessions.

> Do not store up for yourselves treasures on earth, where moths and vermin destroy, and where thieves break in and steal. But store up for yourselves treasures in heaven, where moths and vermin do not destroy, and where thieves do not break in and steal. For where your treasure is, there your heart will be also.
>
> —Matthew 6:19–21

Do you have enough room for all of your possessions? Are there things that you have saved that you do not use? What things can you give away that you do not need? Your generosity can be a blessing to another person, and it can help you in other ways as well.

60. Laziness

Making money as a musician was never easy, but it became especially important when my first child was born. I called several nursing homes to see if I could entertain their residents. Eventually, I was hired to go into different nursing homes every day. I earned much money, and I had fun playing hymns and other songs that the people enjoyed. I entertained elderly seniors at nursing homes more than nine hundred times over the following ten years.

> We hear that some among you are idle and disruptive. They are not busy; they are busybodies. Such people, we command and urge in the Lord Jesus Christ to settle down and earn the food they eat. And as for you, brothers and sisters, never tire of doing what is good.
>
> —2 Thessalonians 3:11–13

Are you a hard worker? Do you believe that you are compensated fairly for the work that you do? If you are not earning enough money, what can you do to supplement your income? Are you able to give some of your income away to people who are not as fortunate as you?

61. Changing History

Shortly after my first child was born, my former landlady committed suicide. Her husband had died twenty years earlier. She told me that her life was never the same after he was gone. I remember the last time that I visited her. As I was driving away, she stood on the back steps of her home and waved goodbye. That was very unusual. I wondered why she was doing that. The next day I went to visit my mother in Minnesota. A few days after I went away, my landlady put her beloved cats in the kennel and took care of everything else that she needed to do. Just before going to bed, she took several sleeping pills. She passed away that evening. I returned from my trip on the day after she died. I entered my landlady's home and called out her name. People who managed her estate were in the living room. They told me the entire story. They said that I could have her piano. I wanted to take it, but I did not have room. My landlady was ninety-five years old when she left this world.

> "Lord," Martha said to Jesus, "if you had been here,
> my brother would not have died."
>
> —John 11:21

Have you ever believed that you could have changed history if you were aware of a particular situation before it happened? Do you believe that God is in control of everything that occurs in this world? Change the things that you can change, but trust God for the things that are out of your control.

62. New Life

People often requested songs when I performed at the nursing homes. One man asked me to play a piece by Mozart. While I was playing the "Rondo alla Turca," the man suffered a heart attack. The ambulance came, and all of the residents went to their rooms. A year later, I returned again to that same nursing home. I was surprised to see that man sitting in the chair where he had his heart attack. When the man saw me, he asked if I could play the "Rondo alla Turca." I was able to play the entire piece that time.

> Now if we died with Christ, we believe that we will also live with him.

> —Romans 6:8

Many people have experienced a time in their life when they could have died, and yet they are alive today. There are reasons why you are living and doing the things that you do. What is your purpose for being alive? How is your life making a difference in the lives of others?

63. Unfading Beauty

I was hired to play the piano at a fashion show. There were beautiful women and cameras everywhere. I played the piano while gorgeous models showed clothes to the people who attended that event. I went home shortly after I had finished playing. I told my wife about the show, but I only had a few details to share. I was able to tell her the name of the designer. She said that he was very famous. I had never heard of him.

> Your beauty should not come from outward adornment, such as elaborate hairstyles and the wearing of gold jewelry or fine clothes. Rather, it should be that of your inner self, the unfading beauty of a gentle and quiet spirit, which is of great worth in God's sight.
>
> —1 Peter 3:3–4

It is important to take care of your body and to dress well. Some people do everything that is possible to look spectacular. Occasionally this can get out of control. God is more concerned with a person's inner beauty. Do you exercise? Are you careful about the things that you eat? Do you seek the approval of other individuals regarding the way that you look? Do you ever treat people differently if they are not attractive to you? What does God see when He looks at you?

64. Generosity

My wife and I wanted to purchase our first home. I needed seven thousand dollars to qualify for a mortgage. My Bechstein piano was worth four thousand dollars. One of my piano students loved that piano. She was willing to pay me seven thousand dollars even though it needed some repairs. My student would have paid more for the piano if I needed additional money. She wanted to help me purchase my house. That student was a very generous person.

> And now, brothers and sisters, we want you to know about the grace that God has given the Macedonian churches. In the midst of a very severe trial, their overflowing joy, and their extreme poverty welled up in rich generosity. For I testify that they gave as much as they were able, and even beyond their ability.
>
> —2 Corinthians 8:1–3

Try to recall someone who was generous to you. Do you consider yourself to be a generous person? What can you do today to bless somebody who has a need? Are you grateful for God's generosity?

65. Fair Compensation

I do not believe that I was paid fairly for one of my performances. I was hired to play for a wedding. I told the bride that my fee would be one hundred and twenty dollars per hour. I met with her to discuss the music and other details. A week later I rehearsed a song with a singer. I drove two hours to get to the wedding. I arrived early. I talked with the florist, the caterer, the photographer, and other people. They all told me that they were being paid very well for their services. It was an elaborate wedding, but it was over very quickly. Just before the bride drove off to the reception in her limousine, she handed me a check. The check was prorated for forty dollars because the ceremony only lasted twenty minutes. I learned many lessons regarding people and business from that wedding experience.

> Do not withhold good from those to whom it is due, when it is in your power to act. Do not say to your neighbor, "Come back tomorrow and I'll give it to you"—when you already have it with you.
>
> —Proverbs 3:27–28

Do you pay your bills on time? What are some reasons why it is important to pay your bills? Do you think God cares about the way that you take care of your finances? Are you paid fairly for the work that you do? How do you treat other people?

66. The Composer

I hired a famous person who wrote music to attend a student piano recital. All of my students performed pieces that were composed by that person. I usually did not play at student recitals, but I played a piece for that special occasion. All of my students were grateful for the opportunity to play their pieces for that composer and to get their music autographed.

> He is the Maker of heaven and earth, the sea, and everything in them—he remains faithful forever.
>
> —Psalm 146:6

Have you ever composed any music? Are you a creative person? How have you used your creative skills? Do you believe that God is the creator of all things?

67. Confidence

I gave my daughter a few piano lessons when she was young. We had fun together. We improvised songs on the black keys. One year she came to my student piano recital. I had not given her a lesson for several months. Just before the concert began, she asked if she could perform on the program. I said yes. When it was her turn, we improvised a piece on the black keys for about two minutes. It went well. I thought that it was brave of her to improvise music in front of a live audience.

> But blessed is the one who trusts in the Lord, whose confidence is in him.

> —Jeremiah 17:7

It takes confidence to perform in front of a live audience. Are you usually a confident person? Can you recall a time when you were not confident? How can you gain more confidence in the future?

68. Guided by the Spirit

Most musicians decide what they are going to play before they get in front of an audience. When I played the piano for parties, I usually chose the next song while I was performing. Occasionally I would look at a person in the audience and be inspired to play a song that I had never performed before. Many times people would come up to me and say that a particular song had a special meaning for them. There were times when I played a favorite love song for a couple on the day that they were celebrating their anniversary. On other occasions, I played pieces that described exactly how a person was feeling. Music can be a very powerful way of communicating with other individuals. I usually found music to be especially powerful when I did not plan what I was going to play.

> But when he, the Spirit of truth, comes, he will guide you into all the truth. He will not speak on his own; he will speak only what he hears, and he will tell you what is yet to come.

> —John 16:13

Are you a person who likes to plan what you are going to do? How do you feel when your plans change unexpectedly? Do you believe that there are reasons things happen in your life? Do you believe that the Holy Spirit can influence you in the decisions that you make?

69. Power of the Grave

My teacher from New Jersey was never completely satisfied with my piano playing. However, one day I played my favorite piece by Robert Schumann for her. She came over to the piano and smiled. I knew that she liked it. I never saw her again after I left that day. I received a phone call informing me that she had passed away. She had taught hundreds of students over the years. Many of them attended the finest music schools in the world. There was never a memorial service or a time to get together with other students who wanted to honor her. There was not an opportunity to say goodbye to the person who had a significant impact on my life. I was with her one day, and shortly after that she died.

> Remember how fleeting is my life. For what futility you have created all humanity! Who can live and not see death, or who can escape the power of the grave?
>
> —Psalm 89:47–48

Nobody lives on this earth forever. There comes a time when everyone passes away. What do you want people to remember about you when your life is over? What do you believe happens to a person after they die?

70. Unexpected Dreams

Piano teachers can influence their students in many different ways. Over time, teachers get to know their students' interests and abilities. All of my students did sight-singing exercises during their lessons. One day I realized that a student had an excellent voice. I told her mother that she was very talented and that the girl had the potential to sing on Broadway. Her mom immediately hired a singing instructor. After a few weeks, that student auditioned for *The Lion King* and was given the role of Nala. One of the girl's biggest dreams unexpectedly came true.

> Now to him who is able to do immeasurably more than all we ask or imagine, according to his power that is at work within us, to him be glory in the church and in Christ Jesus throughout all generations, forever and ever! Amen.
>
> —Ephesians 3:20–21

Try to remember a time in your life when something happened that was better than you could have ever imagined. Some things happen when we do not expect them. Exciting things can happen in your life at any time. Perhaps a "once in a lifetime" opportunity will happen to you today.

71. Sharing Your Faith

The first person I met besides my piano teacher after I moved to New Jersey was a Chinese woman. She was one of the most respected piano teachers in the area. She invited me to her home for a Bible study. I went to her home that evening. The room was full of young Chinese piano students. She shared her faith in Jesus with everyone. I knew that woman for nearly thirty years, but she never mentioned that Bible study to me ever again. Thirty years later, that piano teacher passed away. When I attended her funeral, I wanted to know about the church where the funeral was taking place. I found out that the church originated from that Bible study where I attended many years ago. It was established primarily by the piano teacher's students and their families. All of the teacher's students could play the piano very well, but she believed that it was more important to share her faith with them. The result was a church that had over a thousand people in the congregation.

> When they had finished eating, Jesus said to Simon Peter, "Simon son of John, do you love me more than these?" "Yes, Lord," he said, "you know that I love you." Jesus said, "Feed my lambs."
>
> —John 21:15

What have you done that has had a lasting influence on other people? Do you feel comfortable sharing your faith with another person? How will people remember you when your life on earth comes to an end?

72. Self-Examination

A student of mine played his recital piece in the wrong part of the piano. Every note was incorrect. The student finished the performance and took his bow. After the student had bowed, he said to the audience, "Somebody better get that piano fixed before the next kid comes up here." The student did not realize that he was the source of the problem.

> Examine yourselves to see whether you are in the faith; test yourselves. Do you not realize that Christ Jesus is in you—unless, of course, you fail the test?
>
> —2 Corinthians 13:5

All of us will occasionally fail to recognize our mistakes. It is important to examine ourselves and the things that we are doing. It can be wise to ask somebody to help us with this assessment. Many of our problems get resolved when we simply take the time to make a few minor adjustments. Are you content with the way that you live your life? Are you willing to allow someone else to suggest ways that can help you to become a better person? Try to identify at least one thing that can make your life better.

73. A Jewish Christmas

One of my favorite places to perform was at a soup kitchen on Christmas Day. A Jewish synagogue hosted the soup kitchen every year on this holiday. They sang all of the Christmas carols and brought presents for everyone. Every needy person was able to take home several containers of food. A Jewish trumpet player and I played Christmas carols for an hour. I enjoyed hearing the people sing "Silent Night" and "Joy to the World." Everyone in the room did not have the same religious beliefs, but that did not matter. Christmas at the soup kitchen was a celebration for all of the people.

> For I am not ashamed of the gospel, because it is the power of God that brings salvation to everyone who believes: first to the Jew, then to the Gentile.
>
> —Romans 1:16

What does Christmas mean to you? Have you ever volunteered to help people who had needs? Do you enjoy discussing your faith with people who have different beliefs? Are you interested in things that other people believe? Jesus was willing to talk to anyone.

74. Talents

I was working as the music director in a church when a woman came up to me and insisted that she was going to play the offertory. I did not want to upset the lady, so I said that she could play the following Sunday. The next Sunday I could tell that she was very nervous. She played a hymn very slowly while people collected the offering. It was time to read from the Bible. She continued to play the remaining three verses. Her hands were shaking the entire time. Offertories usually lasted about ninety seconds. That woman played for nearly five minutes. I should have asked her to play for me before I allowed her to perform.

> All these men were under the supervision of their father for the music of the temple of the Lord, with cymbals, lyres, and harps, for the ministry at the house of God. Asaph, Jeduthun, and Heman were under the supervision of the king. Along with their relatives—all of them trained and skilled in music for the Lord—they numbered 288.
>
> —1 Chronicles 25:6–7

What are your greatest talents? How can you use your skills for God in a productive way?

75. Commitment

I was the director of music at a small Episcopal church for thirteen years. I was only absent ten Sundays while I was there. All of the people who attended the church were very dedicated. Blizzards would occasionally occur on Sundays. One of the priests gave his sermon and sang all of the hymns alone when that happened because he believed that God called him to be a faithful servant even if nobody else was present. The church was very tiny, but it was a special place for all of the parishioners. There were times when the people had to make difficult decisions and sacrifices to keep the church open.

> Therefore, I urge you, brothers and sisters, in view of God's mercy, to offer your bodies as a living sacrifice, holy and pleasing to God—this is your true and proper worship.
>
> —Romans 12:1

Have you ever been committed to a particular cause or organization? Why was that commitment meaningful to you? What organization would you like to support today? Now could be an excellent time for you to get involved.

76. Returning Home

I grew up in a small town, the same city where my mother lived for most of her life. I returned several times to visit her. I saw people that I had known ever since I was a child. My mother always told me that I had to play the piano for the residents at the nursing home. People appreciated the pieces that I played. Living in a small town was a pleasant experience. Everyone knew and cared for each other.

> "Return home and tell how much God has done for you." So the man went away and told all over town how much Jesus had done for him.

> —Luke 8:39

Describe your hometown. Do you still live in that city? Who were your closest friends when you lived there? Have you talked to any of those people recently? What was your favorite memory from the time when you lived in that place?

77. My Mother Died

My mom passed away when she was ninety-four years old. She was a devoted wife, and she raised four children. For most of her life, she took care of elderly people as a nurse's aide. For fifty-four years, my mother also went to a nursing home to sing hymns and to read Bible verses to the residents as a volunteer. My mom was very active in her church. She went to help missionaries on the mission field a couple of times for a few weeks. She was the local chairperson for the American Cancer Society. She took care of my two grandfathers in her home when they were old. My mother gave daily care to my father and my brother when they were dying. She served other people throughout her entire life in many different ways. My mom taught me how to help people by using my music abilities. She loved to hear me play the piano. She was always an inspiration to me.

> His master replied, "Well done, good and faithful servant! You have been faithful with a few things; I will put you in charge of many things. Come and share your master's happiness!"
>
> —Matthew 25:21

Is your mother still living? What are your fondest memories of her? Did the two of you have a good relationship? What things did your mom do to help you to become the person who you are today?

78. Music in Heaven

My mom asked me to record forty of her favorite hymns on a compact disc before she passed away. The nurse played the recording for her all day long while she was in hospice care. My mother wanted me to play several of those hymns as a prelude at her funeral. Music was a vital part of her life. Now I believe that she listens to music in heaven.

> And I heard a sound from heaven like the roar of rushing waters and like a loud peal of thunder. The sound I heard was like that of harpists playing their harps.
>
> —Revelation 14:2

Do you believe that you will see your loved ones again someday? If you believe in heaven, what kind of music do you expect to hear when you get there?

79. Rewards

For many years, I had chocolate pianos with M&M's specially made at Christmas for my students. A couple of times I hired an ice cream truck to come at the end of my student recital. I did this to reward my students for their hard work throughout the entire year. Everyone was able to have as much ice cream as they desired. The look on the students' faces when I told them about the ice cream truck was priceless. The truck also helped to make the recital extra special. Students brought their friends because they could get free ice cream. I always looked for new ways to make the piano experience more enjoyable. Chocolate pianos and an ice cream truck were two things that helped me to accomplish that goal.

> Now there is in store for me the crown of righteousness, which the Lord, the righteous Judge, will award to me on that day—and not only to me but also to all who have longed for his appearing.
>
> —2 Timothy 4:8

Have you ever received an award for something that you did? Are rewards meaningful to you? People enjoy the recognition that they receive for their accomplishments. Whom can you reward today? Think about the rewards that God wants to give to you.

80. Different Gifts

A student of mine loved to draw. She enjoyed taking piano lessons, but her real passion was art. I gave the girl a special assignment. I drew ten music symbols on a piece of paper and asked her to create a picture using all of them. I had no idea what she would draw, but she was very excited to do the project. Her finished drawing was full of creativity and imagination. We all have different passions. That girl helped me to realize that there is more than one way to inspire a student to learn about music.

> For just as each of us has one body with many members, and these members do not all have the same function, so in Christ we, though many, form one body, and each member belongs to all the others. We have different gifts, according to the grace given to each of us. If your gift is prophesying, then prophesy in accordance with your faith; if it is serving, then serve; if it is teaching, then teach; if it is to encourage, then give encouragement; if it is giving, then give generously; if it is to lead, do it diligently; if it is to show mercy, do it cheerfully.
>
> —Romans 12:4–8

What is one of your favorite things to do? What are you doing to incorporate that passion into your life? Do you have a desire to use that passion for serving God?

81. Looking Back

I enjoyed going into antique stores to find hidden treasures. One day I saw a box of music in a corner. The music was only thirty-five years old. I was familiar with all of the pieces. When I opened the books, I discovered that they had my markings on them. The music once belonged to a student that I had taught when I started my teaching career. He was an exceptional student. That student did not spend time on a cell phone or with video games. He practiced for at least an hour every day. Over the years, it became harder to get students to practice because other things captivated their attention.

> Do not say, "Why were the old days better than these?" For it is not wise to ask such questions.
>
> —Ecclesiastes 7:10

Do you ever wish that you could go back to an earlier time in your life? Are there changes that you would make? Realize that those days are over. It is not helpful to think about them, especially if they are upsetting to you. Make practical decisions today and enjoy your life. That is what God wants you to do.

82. Seeing What Others See

I usually sat on the floor or a pillow when I taught young children how to play the piano. I wanted to get down to their eye level. I wore comfortable clothes so that I could shuffle around quickly. I was amazed when I looked up at the music from that lower level. I saw the music differently. I loved to experience the piano lessons from my students' perspective.

> In your relationships with one another, have the same mindset as Christ Jesus: Who, being in very nature God, did not consider equality with God something to be used to his own advantage; rather, he made himself nothing by taking the very nature of a servant, being made in human likeness. And being found in appearance as a man, he humbled himself by becoming obedient to death—even death on a cross!
>
> —Philippians 2:5–8

Do you ever try to look at life from another person's perspective? Does this help you to know them better? Jesus is God, but He wanted to experience the same things that we experience. He understands all of the challenges that we face every day.

83. Seasons

As sure as the leaves changed in the fall, some things always occurred at the same time every year in my piano studio. September brought excitement because all of the students received new music. December brought holiday songs that were fun to play. January came, and the winter set in. The winter slump began to arrive. Progress became slow and tedious. However, the middle of March and April always brought new life when the temperature got warmer and the snow began to melt. There was a renewed desire to play the piano amongst my students. Practicing and progress increased dramatically. Everyone began to get excited about the spring recital. It was always important for me to remain positive throughout the entire year. There were times when students lost some of their desire to practice. That was common, but there were other times when practicing would always get better.

> There is a time for everything, and a season for every activity under the heavens.
>
> —Ecclesiastes 3:1

Are there certain times of the year when things get easier or harder for you? How does that affect your mood or your behavior? Try to keep track of when these changes occur. Life is full of seasons. If life is difficult for you today, it will get better for you tomorrow.

84. Encourage One Another

I had a student who was not sure if he would ever be successful. He decided to take piano lessons from me when he was sixteen years old. I encouraged him in many different ways. His confidence improved significantly. He was a student of mine for only two years. I lost contact with him when he went off to college. Fifteen years later I saw him again. He had his doctorate and a very powerful job in the medical field. Piano teachers do not just teach students how to play music. I believe that I helped that student in a small way to have a better life.

> Therefore, encourage one another and build each other up, just as in fact you are doing.
>
> —1 Thessalonians 5:11

How have you been able to influence the life of another individual? People can benefit from the talents that you have to offer. Find a way to affect a person who is in your life today.

85. The Big Hill

When I started my teaching career and had to ride my bike to my students' homes, I had to ride to the top of a gigantic hill every week to get to one of my lessons. It took ten minutes to get to the top of that hill. Thirty-five years later I was on that same hill. I had not been on that hill since I taught that student. I began saying to myself, "You can make it. You can make it." I laughed when I realized that I was saying this to myself while I was driving up the hill in my car.

> A voice of one calling: "In the wilderness prepare the way for the Lord make straight in the desert a highway for our God. Every valley shall be raised up; every mountain and hill made low; the rough ground shall become level, the rugged places a plain. And the glory of the Lord will be revealed, and all people will see it together. For the mouth of the Lord has spoken."
>
> —Isaiah 40:3–5

What is the greatest hill that you have ever had to climb in your life? Did you make it to the top? What has helped you to climb your hills in an easier way? How can God help you to climb steep hills in the future?

86. Blurry Music

I was asked to perform a composition at a memorial service for a piano teacher who had passed away. The service took place in a large auditorium. I had worked hard to prepare for that performance. The time came for me to go out on the stage. I bowed to the audience and sat down. I adjusted my seat and then I looked up at the music. I noticed that all of the music was blurry. I was wearing my wrong eyeglasses. I put my hands on the keys and started to play. I managed to play the entire piece, but it was not easy for me to see the music.

> So we fix our eyes not on what is seen, but on what
> is unseen, since what is seen is temporary, but what
> is unseen is eternal.

> —2 Corinthians 4:18

The five recognized methods of perception are sound, touch, sight, smell, and taste. Do you know anyone who has lost one of these senses? If you ever lost one of these senses, how would that affect your life?

87. More Than I Ask

Over the years, I noticed that my best students always gave me more than I asked from them. Some of them learned an extra piece of music on their own. Other students would perform for people at their church or a nursing home. Some students would write a music report or make something related to music in an art class. I encouraged everyone to work ahead in their assignment books. The best students always did that. That seemed to be a characteristic of every successful person that I knew.

> Confident of your obedience, I write to you, knowing
> that you will do even more than I ask.
>
> —Philemon 1:21

Do you strive to do your best in all of your activities? What are some things that determine how hard you will work? What motivates you to work harder when you are not interested in something that you have to do? Do you ever work harder to please God?

88. Signed Certificates

In the back of some music workbooks, there were certificates that I needed to sign. The documents confirmed that the student had completed all of the assignments. One student took the accumulated documents and displayed them in her room with the rest of her trophies. The signed pieces of paper were very meaningful to her.

> However, do not rejoice that the spirits submit to you,
> but rejoice that your names are written in heaven.
>
> —Luke 10:20

Do you have any trophies or certificates? Do you display your diplomas or other awards? Let people know what you have achieved. Be proud of everything that you have accomplished.

89. Envy

Occasionally I assumed that I did not measure up to other piano teachers. The other teachers seemed to have more talent or more students. They used all of the latest technology, or they had advanced college degrees. They had beautiful homes with one or two grand pianos. Those teachers had waiting lists and charged higher fees. Some of the teachers seemed like they always had their act together in every possible way. However, I was trying to make a difference in the lives of my students. I took what I had, and I shared it. I had enough skills to guide my students in a positive direction. I could always find somebody who had more talent than me, but I was talented as well.

> A heart at peace gives life to the body, but envy rots the bones.
>
> —Proverbs 14:30

Do you ever get discouraged when you see what other people have? Do you ever feel better than somebody else because you have more than they do? What things can you do to stop comparing yourself with other individuals? Know that God's love for you is greater than anything else that you can ever have. There is no need for you to be envious of anyone.

90. Benefits

Private piano teachers do not get paid vacations or pensions. Many piano teachers are never able to retire. All of those things need to be understood when a person decides to become a piano teacher. My wife was a music teacher at a public school. It would have been hard for my family if my wife did not receive several employee benefits from the place where she worked.

> Praise the Lord, my soul; all my inmost being, praise his holy name. Praise the Lord, my soul, and forget not all his benefits—who forgives all your sins and heals all your diseases.
>
> —Psalm 103:1–3

Would you rather earn more money or have extra vacation time? What is the best benefit that you have received from the place where you work? What benefits have you received from God?

91. My Primary Goal

People took piano lessons from me so that they could learn how to become excellent musicians. I always wanted my students to play well, but that was never my primary goal for them. I used music to teach my students skills that they could use throughout their entire lives. I helped some of them to develop self-esteem. Many students learned how to perform in front of an audience. Other people learned how to set goals or to work well with another individual. Some students learned how to listen or to follow directions. I wanted all of my students to seek excellence. Every student changed in various ways while they studied with me. All of them learned how to play the piano, but they learned other things that were more important. Those were the things that motivated me to become the best teacher that I could be.

> Two are better than one because they have a good return for their labor: If either of them falls down, one can help the other up. But pity anyone who falls and has no one to help them up.
>
> —Ecclesiastes 4:9–10

What have you done to help someone become a better person? What is your primary goal in life? Is your goal honoring to God?

92. Getting Old

I received a photograph of a music teacher that I had not seen for thirty-five years. That person had been one of my teachers in college when she was forty-five years old. The person in the photograph was eighty years old. The lady was not able to care for herself. There was a time when she could play the piano with blazing speed and accuracy. People get old. That is the reality of life that we will all eventually face.

> Stand up in the presence of the aged, show respect
> for the elderly and revere your God. I am the Lord.
>
> —Leviticus 19:32

Do you realize that there will come a time when you will be old? How will you assess your life when you see it drawing to an end? What are you doing today to prepare for the time when you will not be able to work or care for yourself?

93. Friends and Admirers

During my career, I played the piano in front of thousands of people. Those people admired the things that I did. They would come up and thank me for playing their favorite songs. Many of them told me about their experiences when they took piano lessons. I called those people my admirers. Admirers were different from my friends. Many of the people who heard me play did not know me. My friends had a close relationship with me. I enjoyed the gratitude and the praise that I received from the audience, but the intimate relationship that I had with my friends was much more meaningful. I appreciated them both, but finding a good friend was something that I cherished.

> I no longer call you servants, because a servant does not know his master's business. Instead, I have called you friends, for everything that I learned from my Father I have made known to you.
>
> —John 15:15

A relationship with a friend is more intimate than the relationship with an admirer. Many people admire Jesus, but Jesus also wants to be your friend. Is Jesus your friend today?

94. Total Commitment

In my life, I met many professional musicians who did not want to do anything else. The only thing they wanted to be was a musician. Some of them went without food or a place to live for several days. They made sacrifices so that they could afford lessons or have time for practicing. I moved away from my hometown so that I could study with a teacher who lived in another part of the country. I devoted an endless amount of time to develop my skills. I gave up many things so that I could have a music career. It required total commitment from me to make a living as a professional musician. Anyone who is not willing to make that commitment will never succeed.

> Then Jesus said to his disciples, "Whoever wants to be my disciple must deny themselves and take up their cross and follow me."
>
> —Matthew 16:24

Do you love the career that you have chosen? What other careers would you like besides the one that you have now? Are there things in your life that are more important to you than God? God wants your total commitment. He also wants you to enjoy your life every day. Live life to the fullest!

95. Regrets and Sadness

Every pianist makes mistakes. I made several mistakes in my personal life. Those mistakes made me sad. Music was important to me, but it kept me away from things that were more valuable. My performances in the past are over. I have to accept the errors that I made. I had to learn to move on from my regrets and sadness so that I could focus on making better decisions in the future. There is no value in thinking about those regretful performances over and over again.

> For as high as the heavens are above the earth, so great is his love for those who fear him; as far as the east is from the west, so far has he removed our transgressions from us.
>
> —Psalm 103:11–12

What are some of your greatest regrets? How would your life be different if you had made other choices? We have all made mistakes, but God forgives them. Are you willing to allow God to forgive you and to leave your regrets behind? I believe that is what God wants you to do.

96. Virtues

Many musicians have big egos. I believed that I was an excellent piano teacher. I did not desire to get advice from anyone. I knew all of the answers. I thought that my students were fortunate to have the opportunity to study with me. I took pride in everything that I did. At times, I was critical of other piano teachers. In my opinion, I was the best teacher in my area. I had taught for many years before I started to associate with other teachers. When I began to associate with them, I realized that they had skills that I did not possess. I learned many things from them. They taught me how to be more patient with my students. Many of the teachers shared their faith in God with me. I realized that the virtues that God taught in the Bible could also help me to become a better piano teacher. It was unfortunate that I did not learn some of those things earlier in my teaching career.

> Love is patient; love is kind. It does not envy, it does not boast, it is not proud. It does not dishonor others, it is not self-seeking, it is not easily angered, it keeps no record of wrongs.
>
> —1 Corinthians 13:4–5

What are your greatest virtues? How do you use those attributes in your daily life? What are some virtues that you need to develop so that you can become a better person?

97. See the Hands

When I attended piano recitals, I tried to sit on the left side of the auditoriums so that I could see the performers' hands. I was able to hear all of the famous concert pianists. Each of those pianists devoted their entire life to music. It was incredible to see their hands move up and down the keyboard. Seeing the performers' hands made their presentations even more enjoyable. The artists spent endless hours practicing so that they could accomplish their highest goals. I was blessed to hear their talents.

> Now Thomas (also known as Didymus), one of the Twelve, was not with the disciples when Jesus came. So the other disciples told him, "We have seen the Lord!" But he said to them, "Unless I see the nail marks in his hands and put my finger where the nails were, and put my hand into his side, I will not believe." A week later his disciples were in the house again, and Thomas was with them. Though the doors were locked, Jesus came and stood among them and said, "Peace be with you!"
>
> —John 20:24–26

Take a moment to think about Jesus' pierced hands. Do you believe that those pierced hands are for you? Do you need to see His hands before you will believe in Him?

98. Evaluations

Many people have evaluated my piano skills. I had to play for piano juries in college to receive my grades. Over the years, I judged hundreds of students at various events. Some pianists were well prepared while other performers made several mistakes. Being evaluated was a stressful experience, but it was also very rewarding. I enjoyed receiving good scores. I was also delighted to be able to tell other performers that they played well.

> For we must all appear before the judgment seat of Christ, so that each of us may receive what is due us for the things done while in the body, whether good or bad.
>
> —2 Corinthians 5:10

Evaluations happen in our lives every day. Are you usually prepared for your examinations? What can you do to receive better assessments in the future? How do you think God will evaluate your life?

99. Thankfulness

Writing this book gave me an opportunity to reflect on all of the people who have had an influence on my life. Some of those people were my teachers. Other friends and family members encouraged me along the way. I will always be grateful to my students and the people who asked me to play the piano for various events. I am thankful for the composers who wrote beautiful music and the craftsmen who spent their lives building fine pianos. The piano tuners made playing the piano more enjoyable. The audiences played a significant role in encouraging me to practice more. Many people enhanced my life, but I will never be able to thank all of them.

I thank my God every time I remember you.

—Philippians 1:3

Who have been the most important people in your life? How have they made your life better? Reach out to some of those people and tell them that you are grateful for the things that they have done.

100. *Piano Moments*

I did not keep the programs from my performances over the years. I did not take many photographs of my students or retain the programs from the student recitals or information about the students who studied with me. I presented dozens of student recitals—all of which have come and gone. Pictures and programs are good to save, but they can just get lost in a box. Every person has memories that they cherish. I have a host of memories that are very dear to me. I have met many people and have seen many things. There are certain things that I wish I had saved, but now they are gone. They just remain as memories. I call all of those memories *piano moments*.

> I remember the days of long ago; I meditate on all your works and consider what your hands have done.

> —Psalm 143:5

What is your most favorite piano memory? How has that memory changed your life? Did that particular piano moment affect your relationship with God?

The Final Reflection

Have you ever talked to yourself? Did you get an answer? Sometimes I have asked myself a question like, "What should I do now?" Eventually, I made a decision based on the responses that came to my mind. I believe that many of those answers were from God. When I started to write *Piano Moments*, I wanted to write a book that could help other people. After a while, I began to realize that God was writing a book for me. I hope that *Piano Moments* has been helpful to you. Perhaps you have even come to know God by reading this book. That would be wonderful. However, I believe that God gave me this book to change my life.

My life is not over. There are more piano moments that I hope to experience. Everyone experiences special moments in their life. Take the time to reflect on your unique stories. Think of Bible verses and life applications that can relate to your experiences. Ask God to speak to you.

Please share your piano moments with me. I would love to hear from you. My email address is mark@pianocanbefun.com. Thank you for taking the time to read this book. God bless you.

About the Author

Mr. Paulson studied music for one year at Crown College in Minnesota. He received an associate of religious arts degree from Northeastern Bible College and a bachelor's degree in piano performance from Montclair State University. He has performed secular and sacred music as an entertainer and a church musician for over thirty-five years. Mr. Paulson teaches private piano lessons in his students' homes in New Jersey. Some of his students are just beginning, while others are performing advanced repertoire. *Piano Moments* is Mr. Paulson's second book. His first book is called *God's Cycle of Music: A Musician's Explanation of God's Purpose and Meaning for Our Lives.* Mr. Paulson lives in West Orange, New Jersey. He is married to Sondra Paulson. Their three children are Marshall, Elliott, and Heidi.

About the Photographer

Sondra Paulson holds a bachelor's degree in music from Montclair State University and a master's of education degree from Gratz College. She has taught general and vocal music in public schools in New Jersey for almost thirty years. Sondra also has a successful career as a professional photographer. Many people use her photographs in books and magazines. Her photographs are for sale at www.istockphoto.com/SondraP. Sondra lives with her husband, Mark Paulson, in West Orange, New Jersey. They have three children: Marshall, Elliott, and Heidi.